For curious young minds everywhere.

# MASCOT KIDS!

**www.mascotbooks.com**

## Curious Minds & Great Voyages in Science

**For more information, please contact:**
Mascot Books
620 Herndon Parkway, Suite 320
Herndon, VA 20170
info@mascotbooks.com

Library of Congress Control Number: 2021905230

CPSIA Code: PRT0521A
ISBN-13: 978-1-64543-893-9

Printed in the United States

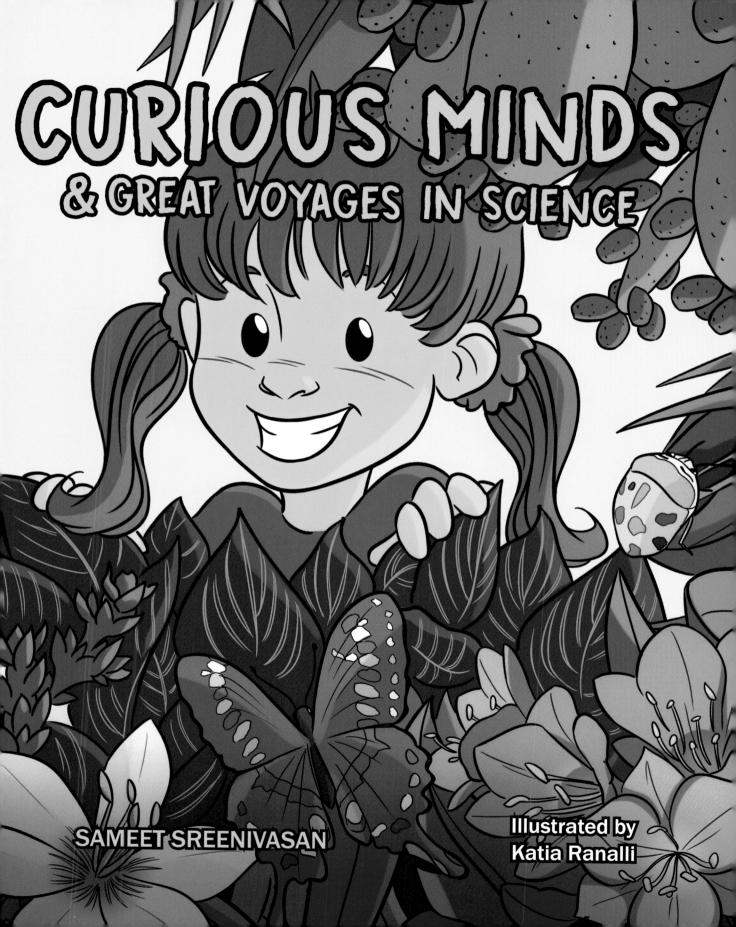

# CURIOUS MINDS
## & GREAT VOYAGES IN SCIENCE

SAMEET SREENIVASAN

Illustrated by
Katia Ranalli

# Jane Goodall
# & the secrets of the
# Chimpanzees

Little Jane, in her reveries,
journeyed far and wide
with her toy chimpanzee, Jubilee,
always by her side.

She knew not as a little child
how certain she could be
that someday the African wild
would be all of hers to see.

But, she held on to her passion,
like her precious Jubilee,
until one day, her actions
led her to Gombe Stream.

There, she camped in patient wait
for the troop of chimpanzees
to watch up close and investigate
their personalities.

For months they shied away in fear
from the stranger in their midst.
But relentlessly, she persevered
until they let her in.

With care she watched the colony
through morning, noon, and night.
And of all their acts and qualities
in her journals she would write.

Like how they'd strip the leaves off twigs
and poke at termite mounds,
and slurp up with a million licks
the teeming bugs they found.

Or how they hugged to show their love
when a troop-mate was in pain,
and wrestled and tickled and pushed and shoved
in lighter moods of play.

When times were tough, Jane still stayed close
and watched despondently
the altercations that arose
between the chimpanzees.

Bit by bit, thus Jane unfurled
the view from where she stood
and shared with us the colorful world
of our cousins from the woods.

So if, like Jane, you wish to live
the scientist's way of life,
observe and be inquisitive
around nature's designs.

There's ants and birds and carnivores
with secrets of their own
that await a curious eye like yours,
forever to be known!

# Isaac Newton
## & the law of Gravity

One summer day, in an old, English town,
Isaac lay under an apple tree,
when a ripened fruit came falling down
and woke him from his reverie.

*Why,* he thought, *did it happen so
that the apple traveled this downward way?*
For surely it had other places to go:
skywards above, edgewise, and away?

Through restless days and sleepless nights,
he pondered upon this mystery
until he found within his sight
a new science of reality.

You see, he said, *it is Nature's rule*
*that every mass attracts another.*
The closer they are, the more they pull.
The heavier they are, the better.

So, the apple—once free from its parent tree—
had no other course of action.
For the Earth tugged harder than anybody
with a keen force of attraction.

So, the next time you jump up off the ground,
throw a ball, or slalom ski,
rejoice in the tug that Isaac found—
the force we call gravity!

# & the theory of Radioactivity

Hello! *Bonjour*!
Behold: Madame Marie!
A trailblazing scientist
as brilliant as could be.

Growing up in Warsaw,
she lived in troubled times,
losing dearly loved ones
to poverty and strife.

But through it all she nurtured
her love for math and science,
learning with a passion,
and feeding her curious mind.

Despite her dreams of college,
she never could enroll.
That, alas, in Warsaw,
was for gentlemen alone.

But onward she persisted,
meeting challenges head-on,
until her efforts won her
a seat at the Sorbonne.

She spent every waking hour
on physics and chemistry,
living and dining simply
on buttered bread and tea.

Then, a strange observation
piqued her curiosity.
'Twas the metal Uranium
beaming X-rays full of energy.

She hunkered down to study
this intriguing property,
devising clever experiments
in her makeshift laboratory.

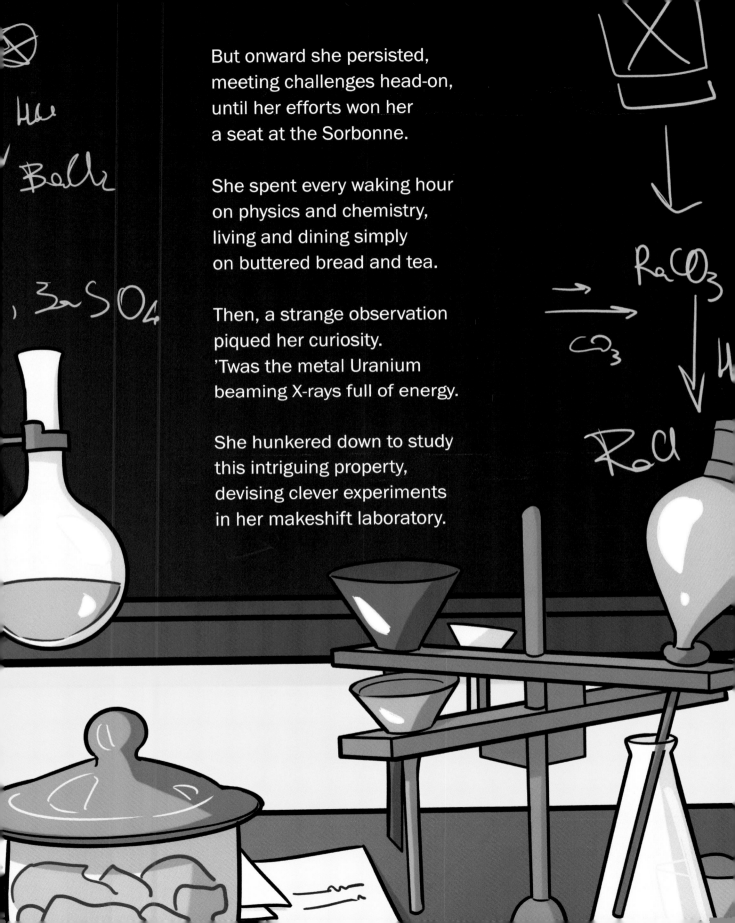

She went on to discover
more radiating entities
and christened this ray-full nature:
Radioactivity.

Her brilliant contributions
won her the Nobel Prize.
So great was her influence
that she won this honor twice!

Thanks to her discoveries,
a doctor can now see
the bones inside our body
by shooting X-rays through you or me.

And next time you take an airplane,
do think of Madame Marie
as your bags get screened
by those magical rays
before your big journey!

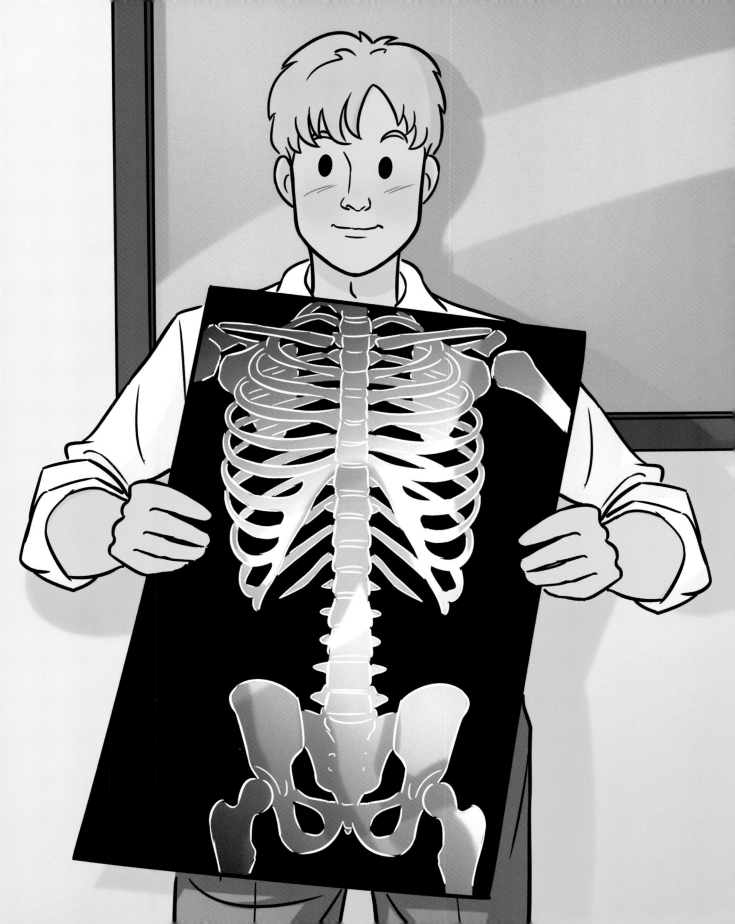

# Neil Armstrong
# & the first landing
# on the Moon

We peered out through the rocket ship and saw the gleaming shore.
How far the moon had seemed to be not many nights before!
Four dusks and dawns had passed on Earth from where we had been thrust.
We'd flown two hundred thousand miles to kiss the ivory dust.

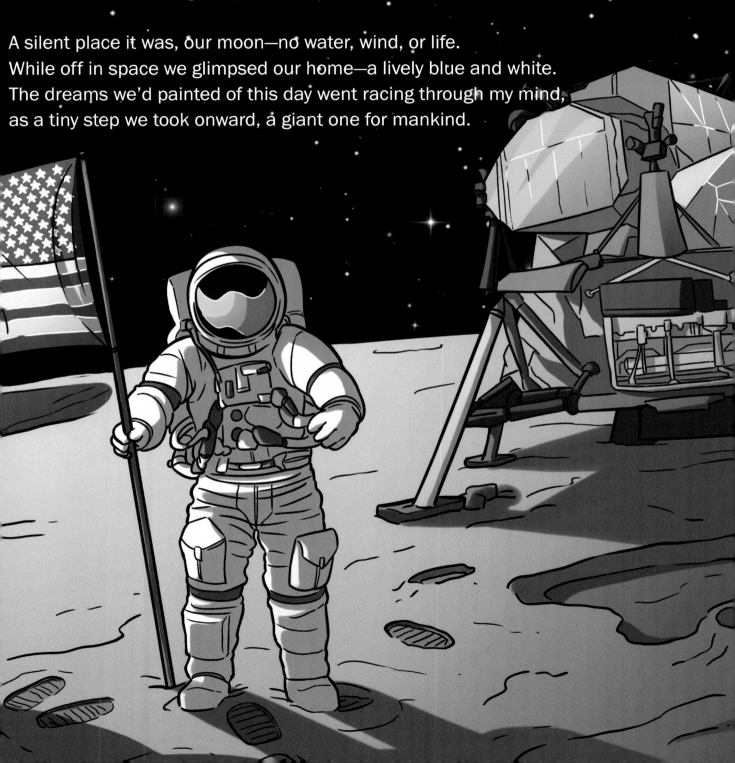

we floated through the sunlit atmosphere as Houston below us cheered.
Millions watched with bated breath as the moon grew ever near.
With gentle grace our Eagle touched down on the tranquil sea.
We crawled out through the narrow hatch into the annals of history.

A silent place it was, our moon—no water, wind, or life.
While off in space we glimpsed our home—a lively blue and white.
The dreams we'd painted of this day went racing through my mind,
as a tiny step we took onward, a giant one for mankind.

# Santiago Ramón y Cajal
# & the discovery of Neurons

There lived in Spain many years ago
a man by the name of Santiago

who took upon himself to explain
the workings of the human brain.

But you'd never have guessed it would be so
if you'd known the school-aged Santiago.

For it was art, not math or science,
that tugged at his heart and consumed his mind.

But his father thought it was unwise
for someone to pursue an artist's life.

And thus set Santiago on a journey
into the world of anatomy

where he found as much to draw and paint
as he peered into a mammal's brain.

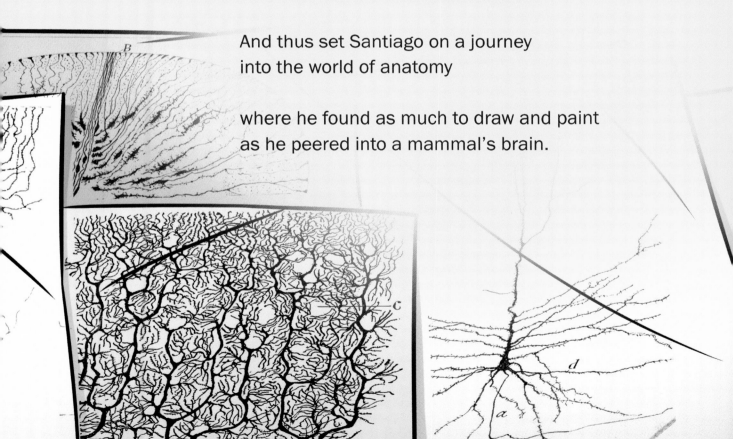

And through his sketches he came to see
the engine that powered our personalities.

The mush that lay inside our minds
was, in fact, many cells of a single kind.

Neurons, we now call these entities,
that knit together like a spider's weave.

And when we hear or smell or see,
they crackle and burst with electricity,

making all our thoughts and actions
as they fire in a chain reaction.

It's not just so for me and you,
but birds and cats and baboons, too.

So when you hear or smell or see,
count, or recite your vocabulary,

do tip your hat to the man from Spain
and behold, in awe, your brilliant brain!

# About the Author

Sameet Sreenivasan has a background in physics and earned his bachelor's and master's degrees in India before receiving his doctoral degree in the United States. He was motivated to write *Curious Minds* to convey how successful scientific exploration takes years of dedication and persistence, even for brilliant individuals like those described in the book. He hopes these stories will inspire budding scientists to dream big and to keep exploring, no matter what obstacles come their way.

Sameet currently works as a data scientist and lives with his wife and daughter in Rockville, Maryland.

 **@CuriousMindsBk**

# Fun Facts

## Jane Goodall

- Jane Goodall had a special bond with the first chimp at Gombe Stream to trust her and let her come close. She named him David Greybeard because of his distinctive silver whiskers.
- Chimpanzees are social animals. They live surrounded by other chimp families along with their own. Chimps can make a variety of expressions with their faces, which comes in handy when communicating with the many members in their community.

# Isaac Newton

- Isaac Newton produced many of his great works of mathematics and physics in a single year, 1666, which is why this year is referred to as Newton's "Year of Wonders."

- Marie Curie discovered two radioactive elements. One of them is named *Polonium* in honor of her native country of Poland. The other is called *Radium*.
- Just like we measure our height in inches and our weight in pounds, we measure radioactivity in *Curies*, named after you know who!

# Neil Armstrong

- Neil Armstrong's footprints on the moon's dusty surface are still preserved today because there aren't any winds (or people or animals) to disturb the moon's surface.

- The moon's pull of gravity is about 6 times weaker than what the Earth exerts on us. This means if you were on the moon (without those bulky space outfits), you could jump a lot higher than you can on Earth.

# Santiago Ramón y Cajal

- Ramón y Cajal was one of the recipients of the Nobel Prize in 1906 for his study of the brain. He also published science fiction stories under the name "Dr. Bacteria."

- There are 86 billion neurons in the human brain—that's about 11 times as many as the number of people there are in the whole world!

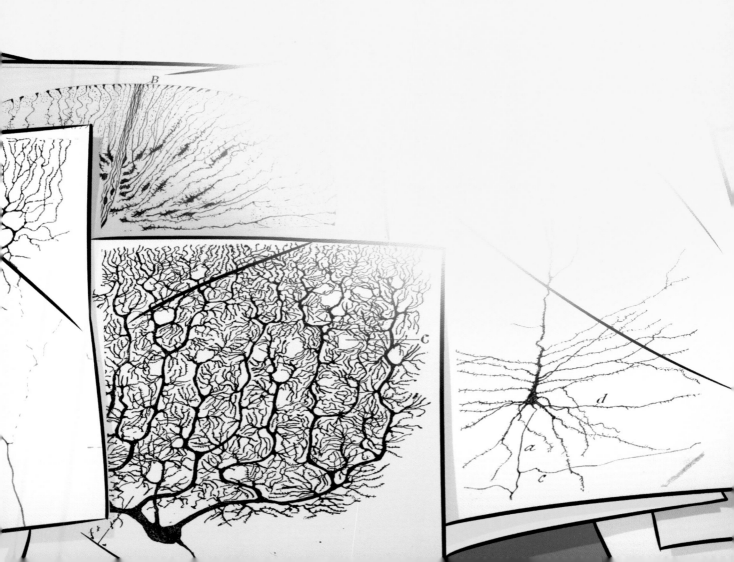